More things I wish I'd said,
and some I wish I hadn't

More things I wish I'd said, and some I wish I hadn't

Collected by
Kenneth Edwards

Abelard · London

ISBN 0 200 72576 9 (hardback)
ISBN 0 200 72575 0 (paperback)

Abelard-Schuman Limited
A Member of the Blackie Group
450 Edgware Road
London W2

Printed in Great Britain by
Robert MacLehose & Co. Ltd
Printers to the University of Glasgow

The Reverend Dr Spooner (the originator of 'spoonerisms') was visiting some friends and was shown into the drawing-room, where a little black kitten was sitting on the table washing itself. Spooner approached the table with the intention of stroking the kitten, but it took fright, jumped off the table and fled. At this moment the lady of the house entered and, after an exchange of greetings, Spooner said that he had found the household kitten sitting on the table and had tried to make friends with it without success.

'When I tried to stroke it,' he said, 'it popped on its drawers and ran out of the room.'

At a dinner party Dr Spooner was asked by his hostess what dish he would like next. 'I think,' he said, 'I should like a little of that stink puff.'

At a formal sherry party at Oxford, a lady with the imposing name of Ironside-Bax saw Dr Spooner, whom she knew, in conversation with a Professor whom she wished to meet. She accordingly approached Spooner and asked to be introduced.

'Certainly, dear lady,' said Spooner. 'Professor, I should like you to meet a friend of mine, Mrs Iron Backside.'

Question:

A motorist travelling at speed bursts through the doors of a public house and fetches up against the bar-counter. Is he liable in damages?

Answer:

Not unless he has his car with him.

'Money won't bring happiness.'

'No, but it will enable you to be miserable in comfort.'

'Mr and Mrs —— have left off clothing of every description, and invite inspection.'

Bernard Shaw was asked for his views on youth. 'I think,' he said, 'that it is wasted on the young.'

Bernard Shaw, who had at one time worked as a music critic, was dining in a restaurant which possessed an excruciatingly bad orchestra. During the first interlude the conductor sent to enquire what Mr Shaw would like the orchestra to play next. 'Dominoes,' replied Shaw.

The Emperor Sigismund, ruler of the Western Empire in the fourteenth and fifteenth centuries, made a speech in Latin which a certain prelate, greatly daring, criticised as ungrammatical.

'I am the Emperor,' replied Sigismund, 'and I am above grammar.'

An aristocratic lady was presiding over a tea party on the lawn of an English stately home. 'If any of you prefer coffee to tea,' she said, 'please don't hesitate to say so; it will be no trouble at all to get the car out and drive down to the village to buy some at the grocers, if he's still open.'

'Who was Salome?'

'She was a lady who took off her clothes and danced before Harrods.'

In an American museum of antiquities, a lady pointed to an ancient Egyptian drinking cup and asked the attendant how old it was. 'Three thousand years and six months, Ma'am,' he replied.

'But how can you measure the time so exactly?' enquired the lady.

'Well Ma'am,' replied the attendant, 'when that cup first came here the gentleman who brought it said it was three thousand years old, and that was just six months ago.'

'Faith, what a terrible thing to say! Sure, if your poor father was alive, he'd turn in his grave!'

About halfway through a tumultuous cocktail party the harassed hostess saw three of her guests coming towards her in outdoor clothes. They had, in fact, only just arrived and had failed to find anywhere to leave their hats and coats, but the hostess assumed that they were about to depart and hastened towards them stammering:
'Oh, must you really stay? Can't you go?'

A letter from a lady to the Ministry of Social Security applying for sickness benefit began with the words, 'I have been in bed with the doctor for a fortnight . . .'

A letter was returned to the Post Office with the following inscription: 'Dead. Address unknown.'

A retired colonel protested indignantly to the editor of a newspaper in which he had been described as 'battle-scared'. The editor apologised and explained that there had been a misprint and that the term used should of course have been 'bottle-scarred'.

A monastic hospital on the continent displayed notices in French, German and English. The English notice read: 'The Brothers of the Misericorde harbour every kind of disease and have no respect for religion.'

'I am dying with the help of too many physicians:' reputedly the last words of Alexander the Great.

An Irishman was asked whether he had any children. 'No,' he said, 'the truth is that infertility is hereditary in my family.'

With what do you connect the name Baden-Powell?
A hyphen.

9

Two monks were drinking tea together, each boasting of the austerities to which he subjected himself.

'For instance,' said one of them, 'I drink tea without two lumps of sugar now.'

'That's nothing,' said the other. 'I drink my tea without six *lumps of sugar.'*

Notice in village café in France:
Persons are requested not to occupy seats in this café without consummation.

Notice in Swiss hotel bedroom: If you have any desires during the night pray ring for the chambermaid.

On the menu of a village restaurant in the German-speaking part of Switzerland:
'Do not leave without sampling the tart of this house.
She is strongly recommended.'

Extract from Malay paper:
'An oppressive heat wave passed over Calcutta yesterday. In the city the temperature rose to the record figure of about 108°. This sudden rise of temperature was responsible for the intolerable heat.'

From advertisement in telephone-book:
'The oldest and most reliable for fur tails of any description. Customers' own tails, broken or otherwise, twisted.'

From newspaper report of sermon:
'Surely the most typically Christian virtue is that of humidity.'

Letter to schoolmaster from pupil's mother:
'Please excuse John from school today as father's ill and the pig has got to be fed.'

From programme of village charity entertainment:
'Shorter address by the Vicar, 4.30 to 6.30.'

From advertisement leaflet:
'Can you afford to be let down nowadays? Then deal with Messrs X Ltd. Branches in most high streets.'

11

Evening paper advertisement:
'Good café chairs and tables; very cheap for cash; also steamer.'

Beneath a photograph:
'Mrs X shooting across a moor pool at her husband's grouse-shooting party.'

From the official programme of a horticultural exhibition:
'Baby Show: best baby under six months; best baby under twelve months; best baby under two years.

'Rules for Exhibitors: all exhibits become the property of the Committee as soon as staged and will be sold for the benefit of the Hospital at the termination of the Exhibition.'

On notice board of village church:
'A special service of thanksgiving for the success of the recent campaign in aid of distressed daughters of the clergy will be held at 6 p.m. and will be followed by mating in the church hall.

A husband had at last prevailed upon his wife to keep a record of her household expenditure and was delighted when she produced her first weekly statement of account. It ran as follows:

Bread, butter, milk, cream, cheese	£3.15
Vegetables	1.75
Tea and coffee	1.10
Meat and fish	3.40
Alcohol	3.65
Petrol	1.32
G.O.K.	3.54
	£17.91

'*This is splendid,*' *said the husband,* '*but there's one thing I don't quite understand. What is the last item: G.O.K.?*'

'*Oh,*' *replied his wife,* '*that stands for God Only Knows.*'

Nervous passenger to air hostess:
'How often do aircraft of this type crash?'
Air hostess: 'Only once.'

Bernard Shaw was strongly in favour of rationalising the spelling of English.

'*After all,*' *he said,* '*if we were consistent we should spell fish "ghoti"; "gh" is pronounced like "f" in "enough"; "o" is pronounced like "i" in "women"; and "ti" is pronounced like "sh" in "nation".*'

Notice in draper's shop:
'If it's quality you want, try us. The best is none too good.'

From a book on first-aid under the heading 'Stings':
'For goat-stings liquid ammonia or vinegar write char-coal in big letters down on her.'

Report on improvements in the telephone service:
'It is now impossible, with the new cables, to maintain an audible conversation over a distance of 3,000 miles.'

Notice in country churchyard:
'Anyone having relatives buried in this churchyard is asked to be so good as to keep them in order.'

Mother of schoolboy to headmaster:
'I want my son to stop learning Spanish.'
'That, Madam, will present no difficulty what-ever.'

Young man writing home from France:
'I left the rather expensive hotel where I stayed when I first arrived and am now very comfortable in a brassiere.'

The vicar said that he thought it would be fitting for the proceedings to be terminated by three jeers for the Queen.

Notice in Swiss mountain hotel:
'Guests are requested not to circulate before 7 a.m. in boots of ascension.'

In Victorian times it was not uncommon for well-to-do people to rent a pew in church. Dr Spooner was among those who did this, and on one occasion when he attended church and approached his pew was greatly annoyed to see a stranger sitting in it.

'I beg your pardon,' he said to the stranger in a low voice, 'but you are occupewing my pie.'

Advertisement:
Don't kill your wife with housework. Let the Hoover do it for you.

A biography of Antonio Vivaldi records that he spent part of his life teaching music in a girls' school and so had many opportunities of experimenting.

Notice in window of lodging house:
'Gentlemen taken in and done for.'

A lady was dissatisfied with the teaching which her son was receiving at Shrewsbury and complained to the headmaster. 'Some of the subjects you teach my boy, French for example, Geography and Mathematics, may be of use to him when he leaves school. But history, ancient and modern; scripture; literature; philosophy: what on earth are they a preparation for?'

'For life, madam, and for death.'

'Don't ever touch those tinned foods that come from abroad. I don't trust foreigners. I believe what my mother used to say: "They eat what they can and can what they can't."'

From a Bournemouth paper:
'Alderman X went on to refer to the dangers which existed in Southbourne, where, he said, you could stand on the road and throw a copper into the sea.'

Advertisement in New Zealand paper:
'Why rend your garments elsewhere when our up-to-date laundry can do the work more effectively.'

From a local paper:
'The baritone voice of Mr X was thoroughly adapted to the "Song of the Vulgar Boatmen".'

From a local paper:
'The motor cycle approached the coroner at thirty miles per hour.'

From a Sale Catalogue:
'These are absolutely new mattresses and are filled with government hair.'

From a Yorkshire paper:
'Pensions for Clergy. Removal of evil principle from parish life.'

A certain professor was asked by a telephone operator to be so kind as to spell his name. 'Certainly,' he replied. 'B for Brontosaurus; R for Rhizophoroceae; O for Opisthothele; W for Willugbaeya; and N for Nucifraga.'

William Pitt the Younger, at the age of twenty-four, had visited George III at Windsor for the purpose of being appointed Prime Minister. The King was doubtful. 'You're very young, Mr Pitt,' he said. 'I think we can rely on time to remedy that, Sir,' replied Pitt.

Work-shy husband: 'I see from the paper that there's talk of another strike.'

Wife: 'Yes, and if you was 'alf a man you'd get a job and go on strike too.'

Extract from a novel of the twenties:

'Young, fair, heart-starved, now and ever, had but one cutlet for the romance that flowed upward from the sunless caverns of her soul.'

Extract from book review in a provincial paper:

'A charming love story—a food story with plenty of thrills.'

Newspaper headline:

'Servants and Burglar. High Court Judge rewards them for bravery.'

From a provincial paper:
'Notice is hereby given that after this date the owners of any fowls straying on land tenanted by Mr X will be destroyed.'

From the Yorkshire Post:
'*The dispensation had to come from the Pope. Now what we both hoped for is actually coming true. Both my wife-to-be and myself were, and still are, true and active alcoholics and we will continue to be so.*'

A Frenchwoman had died and at her funeral her husband bore his bereavement with stoic fortitude, but her lover was in floods of tears.

'Cheer up, old man,' said the husband consolingly. 'After all, I shall probably marry again before long.'

Two Cockneys were on their first visit to the London Zoo and one of them was greatly interested by a bird perched in one of the cages. 'Lor lumme, Bill,' he said to his companion. 'Come and look 'ere. 'Ere's a ruddy heagle!'

'*Not on your life,' said Bill, having inspected the bird; 'it's some kind of a howl.'*

'*Pardon me, gentlemen,' said a keeper who had overheard their conversation. 'That bird is neither a heagle nor a howl. It's a nawk.'*

The first world war was over and the young soldier striding up the village street was on leave pending demobilisation. Just before he reached his cottage he encountered the vicar, who welcomed him warmly and asked him what was the first thing he intended to do when he reached home. 'The first thing I'll do,' replied the soldier, 'is to go to bed with my wife.'

'Ah yes,' said the vicar, 'very natural, I'm sure. And what's the next thing you'll do?'

'The next thing I'll do,' replied the soldier, 'is to get this ruddy great pack off my back.'

Lord Stewart said that when he first became a High Court Judge he seemed to spend most of his time dealing with cases in which collisions had occurred between cars which were both stationary on the right side of the road.

An English lady was entertaining an American officer and was discussing with him British victories and defeats of the past. 'The victory of which I feel proudest,' she said, 'is the British victory which ended the American War of Independence.'

The American could hardly believe his ears. 'British victory, ma'am?' he exclaimed. 'Did you say a British victory?'

'Why, yes,' replied the lady. 'British colonists fighting a German king who employed German mercenaries. What else could you call it?'

Advertisement in local paper:
We tell the truth about our products. They are equal to few and superior to none.

'I'm at my wits' end.'
'Well, you haven't had to travel far.'

An unmarried English lady was staying in a French boarding house and on the morning after her arrival, was asked by her landlady whether she had slept well.
'*Pas très bien, Madame,' she replied. 'Le matelot* etait trop dur.'*
* *Matelot means sailor. The word for mattress is matelas.*

A newly-married young Scotsman was driving away after the wedding 'breakfast' with his bride at his side. Inside the car it was cold, and after a few minutes the young man noticed that his wife was in tears.

'What's the matter?' he asked unemotionally.

'Oh,' sobbed his wife. 'Nobody loves me and my hands are cold.'

The young man considered this. 'The Lord loves ye,' he said, 'and if yer hands are cold, sit on 'em.'

The American Declaration of Independence was, of course, a treasonable document by British law.

'We must indeed all hang together,' said Benjamin Franklin when it was signed, 'or most assuredly we shall all hang separately.'

A nervous young newspaper reporter was interviewing General de Gaulle. 'May I ask you, M. le President,' he said, 'whom you have in mind as—that is to say when—or rather if—'

'Young man,' said the General, 'I think it will save you embarrassment if I assure you that I fully intend to die when the time comes.'

Abraham Lincoln, when authors sent him copies of their books to read used to thank them cordially for the book and add: 'Be sure that I shall lose no time in reading it.'

Extract from a Soviet weekly:

'These are some of the pictures on show at the Young Artists' Exhibition in Moscow's Central Exhibition, one of the U.S.S.R.'s fiftieth anniversary events.

The 1,500 exhibits displayed to best advantage over nearly two acres are the pick of 20,000 submitted by young painters, graphic artists and sculptors in every Soviet republic. Nearly all were executed over the past two years or so.'

Guest at fancy-dress ball, a little the worse for drink, to total stranger:

'*I say ol' man, what are you s'posed to be?*'

'*The wandering Jew.*'

'*Why, thash fine. Let's go and have a drink. I'm a wandering gentile.*'

Wife: 'Here's a letter from those Digby-Joneses, asking us to dine with them again. We really can't until we've had them here.'

Husband: 'Well, tell them so and leave it at that.'

Announcement on notice board of village church:

The Parochial Council of X have kindly agreed that this newly-built Church Hall may be used by us for meetings of our Debating Society, for rehearsals and performances by our Dramatic Society, for choir practice, for meetings of our Theological Discussion Group, for meetings of our Mothers' Union and for rehearsals and performances by our Ladies' Choral Society. The entrance to this hell is at the north end of Park Street, next door to the supermarket.

From a Lincolnshire paper:

Mrs X is again the honorary conductor, and so long as this popular and talented lady holds the reins of the Choral Society there need be no fear of success, either for the Society or any concert that may be contemplated.

Review in Malta paper:
'*They are not dances, but plastic poems, all speaking a language of sensitiveness which the sole alone can understand and appreciate.*'

From a broadcasting programme:
'Symphony Concert. Two pieces of string orchestra.'

At a girls' school reunion, reported by Scots paper:
'*They were all delighted to have Miss X back amongst them. Their best wishes would go with her next week when she set out for her holiday, and they all hoped she would return with*
MEASLES AND WHOOPING COUGH.

From the Andover Advertiser:
Bungalow: 3 bedrooms, lounge, dining-room diner/kitchen, bathroom, coloured suite, toilet 2 miles Andover.

From The Times, *August 1966:*
'*More women needed for random sampling.*'

ITV Programme Change
Southern Television
Sunday July 5, 4.40 p.m. The Big Film
Delete 'The Prime Minister' and substitute 'The Rat'.

For the purpose of the numerous minutes, memoranda and instructions to Ministers which flowed from him during the war, Winston Churchill had two full-time, hand-picked stenographers, and one of these was sometimes required to work until a very late hour. It happened, however, that on one occasion he required both of them to be on duty until after midnight.

'I shall want you both to stay late tonight,' he told them. 'I am feeling fertile.'

A German-born housewife with an imperfect mastery of English was doing her morning shopping and had been asked to pay what she considered an exorbitant price for a cabbage.

'Such much!' she exclaimed. 'You are too dear to me. Round the corner I can become a cabbage for half the price.'

'The house is very quiet,' said a lady to her au pair girl. 'There's not a sound from the nursery. Perhaps you'd better go up and see what Johnny's doing and tell him he mustn't.'

25

Sir Stafford Cripps, a leading member of the first post-war Labour administration, was austere—he was a rigid teetotaller—and deeply religious. In fact there were some who would have accused him of 'dragging religion into politics'. And when Winston Churchill first saw him enter the House of Commons he is reputed to have murmured: 'There, but for the grace of God, goes God.'

Arthur, Lord Balfour, British statesman, scholar and philosopher, visited New York and was shown, among other things, the Rockefeller building. He heard how much it had cost, how many men had been employed in building it, how many windows it possessed, etc.

'Dear me,' he said, 'how remarkable.'

Finally, he was told that the building would last 1,000 years.

'Dear me,' he murmured. 'What a pity.'

A female hypochondriac was seen leaving the doctor's surgery with her face wreathed in smiles.

'You look very happy,' said a friend.

'Oh, I am,' she replied. 'Just fancy! After all this time the doctor has at last found that there's something wrong with me.'

'What's he like, that chap you've been allowing to shoot over your land?'

'Well, he's a man of his word, that I will say. He said anything he shot would be sent to the local hospital, and a friend of mine as well as my keeper have just been driven off in an ambulance.'

A solicitor had defended a flashy blonde against a charge of 'soliciting' and had secured her acquittal. A few days later when he was out walking with his wife, the blonde appeared on the opposite side of the road and, much to his embarrassment, waved affectionately at him. 'And how,' enquired his wife, 'do you come to be on friendly terms with a woman like that?'

'I've only met her professionally,' explained the solicitor.

'Indeed,' replied the wife. 'Whose profession? Yours or hers?'

An atrociously bad golfer was seeking an explanation of his ill success with his opponent.

'I think,' he said, 'that for one thing, I stand too close to the ball before I drive.'

'Maybe,' answered his opponent, 'but if you want my opinion, I think you stand too close to the ball after you've driven.'

What is the difference between Americans and Britons outside their own countries?

The Americans behave as if the place belonged to them. The British behave as though they didn't care who the place belonged to.

According to Derek Heathcote Amory, sometime Chancellor of the Exchequer, there were three things not worth running after: a bus, a woman and a new economic panacea. Why? Because there would always be another one along shortly.

At the age of eighty, Lady Astor said that she had always hated the idea of growing old because of all the things old age would prevent her from doing; but that, having now grown old, she found that the things she was prevented from doing were things she no longer wanted to do.

A timid young curate, having preached for the first time in a church other than his own, stood at the church door, shaking hands with the members of the congregation as they filed out. As none of them even mentioned his sermon he felt more and more convinced that it had been a flop. But he was reassured when one of them, a red-faced farmer, gripped his hand with the words: 'Well done, lad! I didn't get a wink of sleep.'

A schoolmistress was teaching geography in such a fashion that her pupils were bored to tears. But one little boy looked more than just bored. He looked completely blank.

'Tell me,' the teacher asked him, 'do you have trouble hearing me?' 'No,' he replied, 'I have trouble listening.'

Notice at entrance to Japanese hotel:
'Sports jackets may be worn, but no trousers.'

Notice in Japanese hotel bedroom:
'No smoking in bed nor other disgusting behaviour.'

Spanish proverb:
Enjoy yourself. It is later than you think.

An Arab visitor to Britain wanted to be taught how to play golf, but was handicapped by the fact that he knew only two words of English, namely 'yes' and 'no'. In his lessons he did not learn much, since most of the tuition had to be conducted by means of signs. But his English vocabulary was enriched, since he now knew 'yes', 'no' and 'Oh my God'.

Advertisement in New Zealand paper:
'Surgical Instruments: Complete assortment of deceased surgeons.'

Note on hairdressing style:
'A round English tea-bun, high in the centre and fitting close and low to the neck, gives an interesting head shape.'

An official report:
'For some weeks the method has been tried out at the Guildhall by members of the County Council staff. It is now considered foolproof.'

Advertisement in Australian paper:
'Wanted, a second-hand duchess, must be reasonable.'

Young lady in hotel lounge, commenting on buxom lady in frilly, close-fitting costume:
'I wonder how she gets a dress like that into her trunk?'
Male companion:
'And I wonder how she gets her trunk into a dress like that.'

Winston Churchill:
'When you have to kill a man, it costs nothing to be polite.'

An invitation to a dance ended with the words: Dress optional.

'Has your dog a pedigree?'
'Well, he has on his mother's side. And his father comes from a very good neighbourhood.'

Englishman in French restaurant, critically eyeing the meat dish which has just been put before him: 'What is this?'

Waiter (intent on the tune the orchestra is playing): 'A piece of Madame Pompadour, sir.'

Members of the junior class were asked whether any of them could give the name of a play by Shakespeare. Dead silence reigned for a minute, and then a little girl put up her hand. 'Yes, Janet,' said the teacher. 'What name have you thought of?'
'Please miss, Anatomy and Cleopatra.'

Pierre Monteux, famous conductor of the London Symphony Orchestra, was seeking accommodation in a motel for himself and his wife, but was repeatedly turned away on the ground that there was no room. Eventually he came to a motel where the manager, having first said that there was no room, recognised him and called him back.

'I didn't realise who you were at first, sir,' he said. 'You're Someone, and we can always make room for Someone.'

'Everyone is someone,' retorted Monteux coldly. 'I don't think we'll trouble you. Goodbye.'

'Do you believe in striking children?'
'Only in self-defence.'

Notice in New Zealand paper:
'Free Church 11 a.m. "Ahab and the Fishbite".'

'I want a good N.H.S. doctor. You've got one haven't you?'

'Yes, but I wouldn't recommend him. He did me out of a holiday once.'

'How do you mean?'

'Well, I went to him with a terrible crick in the neck and, instead of certifying me unfit for work, he cured me.'

'Lady Winifred left Viceregal Lodge under the Seditious Meetings Act.'

From a sporting paper:
'We had a few years' conversation with Jack Dempsey.'

From an evening paper:
'Newmarket, adorned in all its best summer garbage, is to be visited today and for the next three days.'

A lady resting in a Catholic church saw an old woman shuffle in, curtsey before the altar, cross herself, drop some coins in one of the collecting boxes and then shuffle out again. Half an hour later the same thing happened and this time the lady recognised the old woman as the one who sold flowers at the church door. Leaving the church a few minutes later, she bought some flowers from the old woman and congratulated her on her generosity.

'Oh, so you saw me, did you, dearie?' replied the old woman. 'I always used to pay something to God regular, but I now pay on a commission basis and business is booming.'

From a Newfoundland paper:
'Attached by a silk cord to the bow of the ship was a bottle of champagne which was broken against the side of Lady X.'

A newly-married young man on his honeymoon took his wife to a hotel which he had frequently visited as a bachelor. At breakfast on the first day he asked a waiter (who was a stranger to him) for some honey and, when nothing happened, signalled to the head waiter, who was an old friend.

'I say,' he said. 'Where's my honey?'

After an embarrassed look at the wife, the head waiter replied in an undertone:

'I'm sorry sir, but she doesn't work here any more.'

At a party an American was presented to the Prince of Wales (later King Edward VII) and subsequently expressed appreciation of the easy affability with which the Prince had spoken to him.

'He treated me as an equal,' he said.

'Yes,' said one of his fellow-guests, 'His Royal Highness is always prepared to forget his rank—provided every one else remembers it.'

A prospective passenger by air was asked how much he weighed.

'With clothes or without?' he asked.

'Whichever way you intend to travel, sir,' was the reply.

A married couple were visiting the wife's parents at the seaside.

'*The sea air here is so healthy*', *said the wife's father, 'that it adds ten years to a man's life.*'

The husband, having spent the first three days of his visit sawing wood and clearing scrub for his parents-in-law, said to his wife, 'Your father's right about this place. I was thirty when we came here, and now I feel at least forty.'

A lady was buying a drinking bowl for her dog and was asked by the salesman whether she would like the words 'For the Dog' inscribed upon it.

'I don't think there would be much point in that,' replied the lady. 'My husband never drinks water, and neither my dog nor my cat can read.'

A husband and wife had just seen a film in which Gina Lollobrigida played the lead.

'*I expect,*' *said the wife as they were leaving the cinema, 'you'd be glad to swap me for Gina.*'

The husband considered for a moment.

'*No,*' *he said. 'I shouldn't want to swap you. I should like to have Gina and keep you as a spare.*'

Robert Benchly, the well-known American theatre critic, was called upon in the course of his profession to endure much bad drama and bad acting. Usually, he stuck it out until the end, but on one occasion the play was so bad and the dialogue so trivial that his sense of duty was sorely tried. Eventually, he had his cue. In one scene of the play there was a half-caste girl who spoke the line, 'Me happy, me good girl, me stay.' Benchly whispered to his neighbour, 'Me not happy, me bad boy, me go.'

A black preacher was introducing a colleague to his congregation.

'Brothers and sisters,' he said. 'Dis friend of mine, who's about to take my place in the pulpit, sure is a wonder. He knows de unknowable, he can do de undoable, and—er—he can unscrew de inscrutable.'

Husbands have always had a leisure problem. It's called waiting.

Chancellor Konrad Adenauer, when over eighty, was treated by his doctor for a severe cold.

'I'm not a magician,' said the doctor. 'I can't make you young again.'

'I'm not asking you to,' replied Adenauer. 'All I want is to go on getting older.'

Dr Franz Meyer, Prime Minister of one of the provinces which compose the West German Federal Republic, finding himself obliged to make a speech in English, began with the words:

'Ladies and Gentlemen, I must explain that my relationship to your language is like my relationship to my wife: I am acquainted with it but I have never succeeded in mastering it.'

A nervous old lady, about to travel by air for the first time, and aware that her flight was No. 100, was not reassured when she heard a sepulchral voice over the loudspeaker intone: 'Flight No. 100 is now ready for its final departure.'

A man was examining the household accounts kept by his wife.

'Well, my dear,' he said, 'you'll be interested to know that we've now come to the bridge which we said we'd cross when we came to it.'

Two boys buying tickets for a train journey claimed that they were both under fourteen, and therefore entitled to half fare.

'One of you is over fourteen, and that's for sure,' said the man selling tickets, eyeing the taller of the two.

'No, really,' he replied. 'I'm only thirteen and a half and my brother is six months younger.'

'I don't think it is a good thing that we clergy should wear any kind of clothes,' declared Canon X at a conference of the Church of England Men's Society.

Teacher: 'Why did Othello strangle Desdemona?'
Pupil: 'Because he thought she had been playing the trumpet in his bed.'

A woman's place is in the wrong. (James Thurber)

Bernard Shaw was showing a friend a bust of himself made by Rodin:
'It's a funny thing about that bust,' he said. 'As time goes on it seems to get younger and younger.'

'What are the four most agreeable words to find in a letter?'
'Enclosed please find cheque.'

Aged aunt despondently to nephew and his wife with whom she lives:
'Well, I shan't be a nuisance to you much longer.'
'Nonsense, Auntie, of course you will.'

Young lady adoringly to distinguished writer:

'Dear Mr X, I hear that a book of your personal letters is going to be published.'

Distinguished writer:

'Posthumously, my dear young lady, posthumously.'

Young lady (not quite sure what posthumously means):

'Oh, how thrilling! I do hope it will be soon!'

Doctor: 'Does your husband drink?'

Wife: 'He takes a drink now and then just to steady himself, doctor.'

Doctor: 'And this has no harmful effects?'

Wife: 'Well, there are times when he gets so steady that he can't move.'

A dinner was being given in honour of Miss Diana Dors by friends and admirers. At the end of the dinner, but before the champagne was exhausted, a distinguished actor rose to propose the toast of the guest of honour.

'I cannot claim to know Miss Dors well,' he said, 'but I should like to, and when I met her this evening, she positively gave me the eye and I could see her saying to herself: "There's a man I should like to be made love to by." '

At this the guest of honour rose in her seat.

'I protest', she said, 'at what the speaker has just said. He knows perfectly well that, even when talking to myself, I should never end a sentence with two prepositions.'

A lady arriving at a recently built Irish railway station found that the town which was her destination was three miles distant.

'Why couldn't you have built the station a little nearer the town?' she enquired of the station-master.

'Well, ma'am, we did think of that,' he replied, 'but on the whole we thought we'd better keep it near the railway.'

'How would you define a bore?'

'Someone who, when you ask him how he is, tells you.'

Mother to marriageable daughter whom she has so far failed to 'get off':

'Maybe I was wrong. Perhaps you ought to play easy-to-get.*'*

'What is anatomy?'

'Something which we all have but which looks best on a girl.'

'What to you is the most musical sound?'

'The sound of someone else washing up.'

'What makes a pessimist?'
'Financing optimists.'

*'What does every red-blooded young American want to be
when he grows up?'*
'Rich.'

A young student at Oxford was attending a lecture
which bored him, and after about half an hour he
rose from his seat without a word to the lecturer,
pushed past his neighbours and made for the door.
He had nearly reached it when the lecturer called
after him:
'Mr X! Come back! You've forgotten something.'
'What?' enquired the departing student.
'Your manners,' replied the lecturer.

*One of the numerous boroughs of which London was
formerly composed—an East End borough—was organising
a pageant in aid of a local charity, and it was considered
essential to include in it a part for the Mayor which should
be sufficiently impressive and take into account the fact that
His Worship was a Cockney born and bred. After much
discussion the pageant committee decided to include a riot
scene in which the Mayor, disguised as King Henry VIII,
would come forward and, in a voice of authority, exclaim
'Silence,' whereupon the rioting would cease. The Mayor
was delighted with his part, which he rehearsed frequently
in the privacy of his home, but when the day of the pageant
dawned, he began to feel apprehensive and, when the
moment came for him to make his entry, he strode forward,
raised his right hand and shouted in stentorian tones, ''Ush.'*

41

When a boy in his late teens borrows his father's car he subtracts five years from the life of the car and adds the same number of years to his father's age.

A woman driver is one who drives in exactly the same way as a man driver does and gets blamed for it.

Managing Director to secretary: 'Now Miss Jones, take a threatening letter.'

On the sunlit lawn of the park only two seats remained vacant: one of the comfortable deck-chairs and, close beside it, one of the uncomfortable wooden benches. Two people were making for the deck-chair: a fragile-looking old clergyman and a stout, middle-aged woman who easily overtook him. As she settled herself in the deck-chair she turned her head to see the old clergyman seating himself on the wooden seat, and called out to him, 'God helps those who help themselves.'

Almost immediately afterwards there was a rending sound and the deck-chair, unable to bear the stout woman's weight, collapsed, leaving her sitting on the ground. The old clergyman forbore to smile but said in an audible murmur,
'The Lord giveth and the Lord taketh away.'

Notice on temporarily unattended fruit barrow:
God help those who help themselves!

Labour Candidate: 'What are we to do about crime?'
Conservative heckler: 'Nationalise it! Then it will
never pay!'

The art of conversation isn't lost. It's hidden
behind the TV.

'I wonder, Lady Newrich, if, when I come to your party
tomorrow, I could bring Mr X the well-known organist and
composer, who is staying with us?'
'Why, of course, and please tell 'im to bring 'is
instrument with 'im.'

In a small shop in Portobello Road there were
many second-rate portraits of people in Edwardian,
Victorian and Regency dress.
'What are those?' said a customer, pointing at the
portraits.
'Ancestors,' replied the shopkeeper.
'Whose ancestors?'
'Anyone's as 'as a mind to buy 'em.'

Slightly inebriated hostess bidding farewell to equally inebriated guest:
'Goodbye. It was so kind of me to invite you.'
Guest:
'Not at all, not at all. It was so kind of me to come.'

An ill-informed Cockney showing his wife and family round the Natural History Museum, indicates a case containing a stuffed ostrich.
'This 'ere,' he says, 'is the hostrich, now extinct.'
Wife: 'But surely, dear, the ostrich isn't extinct?'
Husband: 'Well, this one is.'

The man who was later to become Napoleon III, Emperor of the French, fled, in 1846, to England, where he received much generous hospitality from a certain Lady Blessington. After he had returned to France and become Emperor, Lady Blessington visited Paris and met him at a reception, where he treated her coldly and asked, in a condescending fashion, how long she expected to remain in France. 'Deux mois, Majesté,' she replied, 'et vous?'

Extract from *The Freethinker:*
'Although Mr Barnet had expressed a wish to be cremated, we understand that he was buried with a clergyman.'

From the Windsor Express*:*
'Hundreds use our service. They know no better.'

Seen in the *Evening Post:*

'Mr Wedgwood Benn said, ". . . there is a great revolution under way in education. My education policy is to raise the school leaving age to 65." '

From the Morning Telegraph *:*

'I spent several days in a mental hospital and felt completely at home,' Christopher Mayhew, M.P., told a meeting of the Sheffield Branch of the Mental Health Association.

From the *Evening Standard*:

'There had been a slight hitch when it was discovered that Williams had arrived without his pants. He was, however, accompanied by his father-in-law, a bishop in the Evangelical Church.'

Conrad Eden, the organist of Durham Cathedral, was awarded an honorary Doctorate of Music. Later, after he had retired to a village in southern England, and had become known locally just as Dr Eden, his telephone rang one day while he and his wife were out. The call was taken by their "daily" woman, who heard an anxious voice inquire: 'Is Dr Eden there? My husband isn't well and I should be very grateful if the doctor—'

'Oh,' interrupted the "daily", 'you're making a mistake. Dr Eden isn't the sort of doctor that could do anybody any good.'

A Catholic Irishman was discussing a local High Church Anglican priest, whose parishioners commonly addressed him as 'father'. 'Him a father!' said the Irishman disgustedly, 'and him a married man with a wife and two children!'

A little girl, having said all her usual prayers—'Bless and take care of Daddy and Mummy and Nanny,' added: '—and please, God, take care of yourself. 'Cos if anything happens to you, we're sunk.'

A wounded Nazi pilot who had been shot down over England and was being treated in a British hospital spent most of his waking hours extolling the doctrines of the Third Reich and abusing its enemies. It was eventually decided that a blood transfusion would be necessary and, when this had been carried out, the doctor patted the man paternally on the shoulder and said:

'There you are my lad. You've got two pints of good Jewish blood in you. Let's hope it improves your manners.'

A man was accused of deserting his wife and leaving her without means of support. 'Judge,' he said, 'you don't know my wife. If you did, you'd realise that I'm not a deserter. I'm a refugee.'

An American small farmer had just been to the poll and was asked how he had voted. 'Well,' he said, 'on my way there I met a Republican who said he'd give me ten dollars if I'd vote for his party; so I took the money. Then I met a Democrat who said he'd give me five dollars if I'd vote for his party; so I took his money too.'

'So you voted Republican?'

'No, I voted for the Democrats. I figured that they were fifty per cent less corrupt than the Republicans.'

A High Court Judge, summing up in a divorce case, criticised the behaviour of the younger generation. 'Time and again,' he said, 'I hear of young men and young women devoting to drinking, dancing and even gambling, time that would be much better spent in bed.'

From an evening paper:

'A competition is to take place to determine the owners of the best three pairs of legs in Vienna.'

From a local paper:

'There were over two hundred dancers present, amongst whom we noticed the Mayoress and her two tons.'

A newly married, newly commissioned junior naval officer who had worn his uniform for the first time the day before, was invited to attend an important reception given by no less a person than the First Sea Lord of the Admiralty, a full Admiral with bushy eyebrows and a reputation for ferocity. When the young man, accompanied by his young wife, arrived at the reception, they found that they had to wait their turn to be greeted by their formidable host; and while they waited the young man was overcome by stage fright. Ought he to begin by introducing his wife to the Admiral or by introducing himself? Ought he to thank the Admiral for having invited them, or postpone this until the time came for their departure? He was still dithering when the dread moment came and he was horrified to hear himself blurt out the words: 'Darling, this is my wife.'

The Admiral eyed him keenly: 'Young man,' he said, 'you deserve to be courtmartialled for cowardice in the face of the enemy. But as your wife is the prettiest girl in the room'—and here he took her by the shoulders and kissed her smartly on both cheeks —'we'll say no more about it.'

A French scientist who was suffering from what proved to be his last illness was asked whether he had made his peace with God.

'Why,' he replied, 'I don't know that we've ever quarrelled.'

'The world will never starve for want of wonders, but only for want of wonder.' (G. K. Chesterton)

'It's easier to fight for one's principles than to live up to them.' (*Alfred Adler*)

An emotional young man had spent at least an hour and a half telling an older woman friend about his many troubles.

'It's wonderful of you to listen to all this,' he said, 'I had a splitting headache when I came, and now it's gone.'

'It's not gone,' was the reply, 'I've got it!'

From a Scots paper:
'Every man employed by the Corporation would be un-employed, unless he were employed by them or by somebody else.'

The President of the United States is ex officio Commander-in-Chief of the armed forces and it was in this capacity that, during and after the Civil War, Abraham Lincoln received petitions and appeals of all kinds from officers and men. Such petitions and appeals were normally accompanied by letters of recommendation from persons in high places, but in one case, that of a humble private applying for leave to visit his mother, this was not so.

'Has this man no friends in high places?' enquired Lincoln of his Private Secretary.

'Evidently not, sir,' replied the Secretary.

'Well then, let me be his first,' said Lincoln, and marked the application 'Approved, A.L.'

As a small boy, the great J. D. Rockefeller was being severely beaten by his mother, a strict disciplinarian, for an offence he had not committed. Before the beating was over, the boy convinced his mother of his innocence, but she continued beating him with the following words:

'I may as well finish now I've begun. But it will be credited to your account next time that you're naughty.'

If you can't make light of your troubles, keep them dark.

A man who had sacked a servant for laziness was asked to give him a reference. After much heart searching he wrote:

'If you can get X to work for you, you will indeed be fortunate.'

Advertisement in Irish paper:
'Deno's—stocks practically all the leading brands of liquor. Funerals undertaken at short notice.'

Advertisement in Scots paper:
'Piano to suit beginner with legs.'

During a storm at sea, one of the passengers, a lady, asked the captain: 'Are we in great danger?'

'We are in the hands of God, madam,' he replied.

'Oh dear!' exclaimed the lady. 'Is it as bad as that?'

A minister of a sect for whom baptism involved total immersion asked a recent convert whether he had ever been baptised.

'Yes,' he replied, 'by an Anglican clergyman when I was a baby.'

'Brother,' said the minister, 'for us that ain't baptism. That's just dry-cleanin'.'

Abraham Lincoln was discussing with a friend the merits of a certain historian.

'I do not think,' said the friend, 'that any historian has ever plunged so deeply into the fount of learning.'

'Or come up so dry,' rejoined Lincoln.

A young man sent his beloved eleven roses, together with a note which read: 'I had in mind sending you twelve roses, but decided that eleven would suffice. You yourself are the twelfth.'

At a social gathering during the Civil War Abraham Lincoln let drop a few words in praise of the South. A lady who heard him was shocked and exclaimed:

'How can you speak kindly of your enemies, whom you ought to destroy?'

'Madam,' replied Lincoln, 'do I not destroy them when I make them my friends?'

'How sweet she looks as a bride!'
'Yes, she always does.'

For the aged it is not feeling old that is the tragedy. The tragedy is not feeling old. (Attributed to H. G. Wells)

'I like work. It fascinates one. I can sit and look at it for hours.' (Jerome K. Jerome)

Leaving an evening party, Groucho Marx said to his host:

'I've had a wonderful evening, but this wasn't it.'

During the German occupation of Denmark in the Second World War the courageous King Christian saw the Nazi flag flying over a Danish public building. He immediately telephoned the Commandant of the German occupying forces and asked for the flag to be taken down. The Commandant refused.

'Then a soldier will go and take it down,' said the King.

'He will be shot,' said the Commandant.

'I don't think so,' replied the King. 'I shall be the soldier.'

The flag was removed.

Extract from the *U.K. Press Gazette*:

'*Blackburn Times* reporter Valerie will not forget the night she danced with Prime Minister Edward Heath at a Young Conservatives Ball—and ended up in the maternity ward of the local hospital.'

Advertisement:

The Royal Academy of Rats
Dante Gabriel Rossetti
Painter and Poet
Last two weeks

In a tiny European state several men had been sentenced to imprisonment and were lodged in the small building which was the state's only jail. As time went on the cost of guarding and feeding the prisoners became too much of a burden, and it was eventually decided that, since the men were all qualified artisans, they should be released on parole during the day in order that they might earn their keep. They had, however, to be back in time to be locked up by 10.30 p.m. and all went smoothly until one of them returned too late. The jailer, who was tired and wanted to go to bed, was furious. 'Kindly remember,' he said, 'that you are a prisoner. If you ever do this again, I shall *lock you out*!'

From the Evening Standard *:*
'*As the war faded and peace loomed Vera Lynn was able to advise her husband and business manager, Harry Lewis, that she was going to have a baby. It is a symbolic and logical climax to five gruelling years as a "Forces Sweetheart".*'

Official statement by Scottish Home and Health Department:
'During Nuclear Attack there will be a School Holiday.'

Report in The Times :
'*An RSPCA inspector commended Mr Peter Humphrey for saving a goldfish from drowning.*'

Report in the *Daily Mail :*
'President Nixon sets off today on a tour of six Asian nations to explain his intentions and assure the countries that America is abandoning them to their enemies.'

Vicar's announcement in Parish magazine :
'*The headmaster of* —— *School will preach at the Parish Church on Sunday, May 13th, and another of the staff on May 6th. On both of these Sundays I hope to be away on holiday.*'

On the outbreak of the American Civil War President Lincoln directed that he should be kept fully informed of everything that happened on the various fronts.

In obedience to these instructions General McClellan sent him a telegram which read, 'Have captured six cows. What do I do now?' Back came the reply from the White House, 'Milk them.'

Edwardian dowager: 'Yes, I'm always kind to girls. One never knows who they may become.'

Sir Oswald Mosley, leader of the British Fascists (the 'blackshirts') was to speak at a meeting attended by numbers of his supporters as well as by some of his bitterest opponents. To the accompaniment of cheers from his supporters, he mounted the rostrum with great dignity and, standing to attention, gave the fascist salute (identical to the Nazi salute) by raising his right hand in the same way as a schoolchild raises its hand if it wishes to speak to its teacher. This was followed by thunderous applause from his supporters, but as soon as it subsided a voice in the crowd shouted 'All right, Oswald. You may leave the room.'

A patient was concerned about his heart:
'Don't worry,' said his doctor, 'your heart will last as long as you live.'

'Pay court to every woman you meet. Even if you get no more than five per cent out of it, it will be a good investment.' (Anon.)

According to Chapter 22, verses 16–21 inclusive of St Matthew's Gospel, Jesus of Nazareth was asked by emissaries of the Pharisees whether it was lawful to pay tribute to Caesar. If he had answered 'Yes' he could have been denounced as a pro-Roman; if he had answered 'No', he could have been accused of sedition. Instead, he asked to be shown a coin and enquired whose 'image and superscription' appeared on it. They replied that it was Caesar's, whereupon he said:

'Render therefore unto Caesar the things that are Caesar's and unto God the things that are God's.'

In other words: your question is a purely political one and nothing to do with religion.

The Reverend Dr Spooner was interviewing a student who, it was reported, had grossly neglected his studies. 'I am afraid, Mr X,' he said, 'that the reports on your work are far from favourable. In fact, I do not think I should be going too far in saying that you appear to have tasted the whole worm.'

Large parts of Scotland were covered by snow and numbers of people, including members of the Red Cross were hard at work clearing roads and digging their way to isolated cottages. One member of the Red Cross team, having penetrated to a tiny cottage in which an old lady was known to be living alone, knocked at the door, which was promptly opened by the old lady.

'I'm from the Red Cross,' panted the young man, 'and I've come to ask you whether . . . .'

'Listen young man,' broke in the old lady, 'I know the Red Cross is a good cause, but I subscribed to it only six weeks ago. I can't afford to give you any more now.'

Mother to sixteen-year-old daughter:

'Tell your boy-friend he must bring you back here by ten and not a minute later.'

'Oh mother, I'm not a child any longer.'

'I know. That's why I want you back here by ten.'

'What is a psychiatrist?'
'A man who tells you what you already know in words you can't understand.'

A business man received a telephone call from his wife while he was at his office. 'There's something wrong with the car,' she said.

'What?' enquired her husband.

'Well,' replied his wife in a small voice, 'for one thing there's water in the carburettor.'

'All right,' said the husband, 'I'll send someone to fix it for you. Where is the car now?'

'Well, as a matter of fact,' said his wife in a still smaller voice, 'it's in the river.'

'What do you consider to be one of the greatest consolations of your profession, vicar?'

'The fact that, in the presence of my wife, my children and members of the public I can, for a limited period of time every Sunday, say whatever I like on any subject without being interrupted or contradicted.'

'What is the fifth commandment?'

'Humour thy father and thy mother.'

A young woman who had just accepted a proposal of marriage from an actor said that she hated to think of his having been married three times before, and of the reasons for his three divorces.

'Come, my dear,' he said, 'you mustn't listen to a lot of old wives' tales.'

Sunday School teacher: 'What happened on Ascension Day?'

Pupil: 'We had cream buns for tea.'

Victorian young lady: 'I am afraid I allow myself to be carried away by my enthusiasms.'

Victorian young man: 'If only I were one of them.'

The ex-trainer of a heavyweight champion was criticising his former employer. 'You ought not,' said his companion, 'to say such things about him behind his back.'

'I know,' said the other, 'but believe me, it's the only safe way.'

A little boy had been told by his mother that, whenever he was tempted to do wrong, he should say 'get thee behind me Satan' and that this would help him to resist temptation.

Soon afterwards he was caught in the larder stealing jam, and his mother demanded sternly whether he had done what she had told him to do and said 'get thee behind me Satan'.

'Yes, Mother, I did,' replied the little boy, 'and Satan got behind me and pushed me in.'

Before the days of the breathalyser, a motorist, somewhat the worse for drink, was driving erratically along a country road in thick fog and collided with something, of which all he could see was that it had a black body and a ring of white round its neck. The creature, whatever it was, disappeared into the fog and the motorist continued on his course until he saw the lights of a public house. He and his passenger promptly descended and, after ordering drinks, asked the barman whether anyone in the neighbourhood owned a very large black dog, or a black bull or cow, with a ring of white fur round its neck.

'No,' said the barman, 'no animal of that sort hereabouts.'

'Well,' said the motorist to his passenger, 'it looks as if you were right. It *must* have been the vicar.'

Mistress (*hearing the front door bell ring*):

'*Go and see who that is, Mary. If it's Mrs A tell her I'm not at home.*'

Maid (*later*):

'*It was Mrs A, Ma'am. I told her you weren't at home and she said she was very glad to hear it.*'

An Englishman on a walking tour in Ireland asked one of the natives how far it was to the next village.

'Only about half a mile, your Honour,' was the reply.

But in fact the journey took nearly three hours and when the Englishman reached his destination he was tired out and footsore. On his way back next day he happened to meet again the man who had misled him and demanded an explanation.

'Why now,' replied the Irishman, 'I meant no harm at all. 'Twas just that I wanted to give your Honour a pleasant answer.'

A speaker at a political meeting was being constantly interrupted by a heckler who shouted mockingly: 'Tell them all you know. It won't take long.'

After the third interruption the speaker shouted back: 'I'll tell them all I know, if they want me to; and I'll tell them all you know, too. It won't take any longer.'

Clergyman to mutinous daughter:

'You're very aggressive, my dear. Remember—"the meek shall inherit the earth".'

'Oh yes, I dare say they will—when the others have done with it.'

Employer to gardener:

'How is your wife's pneumonia now, Robinson?'

'She's still a bit weak, sir, but the peumonia has gone, thank God.'

'Peumonia? It's pronounced neumonia. Didn't you hear me say neumonia?'

'Yes sir, but I didn't like to correct you.'

The expansive stranger addressed the little man who was the only other occupant of the railway carriage. 'You will be interested to know, sir,' he said, 'that in the luggage rack above your head there is a case containing a quantity of the most powerful explosive yet known to man. I invented it and am on my way to have it tested at a government research establishment.'

'But—but suppose it goes off?' said the little man.

'Then sir,' was the reply, 'it does not matter. The secret dies with me.'

A middle class English girl visiting relatives who owned a cattle ranch in the far West of the USA, fell in love with and married one of the cowmen and at the first opportunity brought him home to meet her English parents, having first warned them that John, though a wonderful guy, was a pretty rough diamond, and that they must make allowances for his primitive manners.

When the couple arrived, in pouring rain, at the home of the wife's parents, she went in ahead of her husband in order to pave the way. 'Where is John?' asked her parents. 'It's all right,' she replied, 'he's just brushing his gums* on the mat.'

* American slang for goloshes.

As is well known, Karl Marx was the author of a book called *Capital (Das Kapital)*, which is the Bible of modern communism. After he died, his widow was asked whether her marriage had been a happy one.

'Yes,' she replied, with a sigh, 'we were happy enough, but I wish dear Karl could have spent some time acquiring capital instead of merely writing about it.'

'Did you say that the proper place for a woman is in the home? You're nothing but a male chauvinist pig !'

'If I said that, I didn't mean to include you. The proper place for a woman like you is in a home.'

A man and his wife were on their way to a formal dinner party in a small open car. As they were late they were going pretty fast, and on rounding a corner, were horrified to see that a tree had fallen across the road. The husband, who was driving, jammed on the brakes, but was unable to prevent a collision so violent that his wife, who was in the back seat, was pitched bodily out of the car in a sitting position on to a clump of thorn bushes.

The husband, shaken but unhurt, telephoned from a wayside telephone kiosk to their prospective hostess, to explain that because of the accident he was afraid they would be unable to attend the party. On the following day the wife, now partly recovered from her painful experience, herself telephoned the hostess to express her regret.

'I know you couldn't help it, dear,' said the other woman, 'but if you knew what it did to my seating arrangements!'

'*Your* seating arrangements!' was the reply. 'What do you suppose it did to mine!'

A timid mother, wishing to explain the facts of life to her two children, Charlie aged eight and Johnny aged seven, did so in the time-honoured way by telling Charlie about the birds and the bees and asking him to pass the information on to Johnny. Charlie agreed and straight away sought out his young brother.

'Hi Johnny,' he said, 'you know all about how babies are born? Well, it's the same with birds and bees, see?'

A lady wrote to the editor of a woman's magazine to ask whether it was good form to wear the latest low-cut, backless swimsuit on a public beach. The answer she received was: 'It is good form if your form is good. If not, not.'

A small boy told his father that, according to what his mother had said, the people who had moved in next door were Lesbians. What was a Lesbian? Father did his best— Lesbians were ladies who liked living with other ladies instead of with husbands— and the boy went away satisfied.

The father then sought out his wife and asked her indignantly what on earth she meant by telling the boy that their new neighbours were Lesbians. 'Lesbians!' echoed his wife. 'I never said any such thing, I said they were Wesleyans.'

'What sort of a crossing was it?'

'I can best answer that by saying that at one moment I was afraid I was going to die, and the next moment I was afraid I wasn't.'

'I don't suppose you've had any breakfast, then?'

'Just the opposite, I'm afraid.'

It was the junior Scripture class and the teacher had asked how Adam and Eve had been punished for their disobedience. An arm shot up. 'Well, Betty?' 'Please Miss, they were both expelled from Eton.'

Two families, one Catholic, the other Protestant, lived next door to each other. Each family had an only child about four years old: the Catholic family a little girl, and the Protestant family a little boy. Each child was told not to associate with the people next door because they were 'different'. Nevertheless the children so obviously wanted to meet and play together that their parents buried the hatchet and, as a first step, the two children met in the Catholic family's garden, where there was an artificial pool.

They spent a happy afternoon splashing about in the pool (being so young they were not required to wear swimsuits) and when they eventually returned to their respective homes were asked by their parents whether they had enjoyed themselves. They said that they had and added that they had never realised before what a big difference there was between Catholics and Protestants.

The catering officer of an Army unit had been able to acquire, at a cut price, a small quantity of caviar which, intending to give the men of his unit a special treat, he included in the menu for their evening meal. Most of the men seemed delighted, but one old NCO, having smeared the caviar on a slice of bread, and eaten a mouthful, seemed disgusted.

'What's wrong?' he was asked.

'Why,' he replied, 'this darned blackcurrant jam tastes like fish.'

A male tennis player in a mixed doubles match threw away a game and set by serving three double faults.

'Sorry partner,' he said, 'I'm not playing my usual game today.'

'What *is* your usual game?' replied his partner.

During the first world war Queen Mary expressed a desire to visit a unit of the Australian forces. The Australians, though magnificent fighting men, were known to have scant regard for social or military etiquette, and one of the Queen's equerries thought it best to approach the colonel of the unit in advance in order to ensure that the proper formalities were observed.

'I assume, Colonel,' he said, 'that your men have been— er—suitably prepared for the occasion.'

'Sure,' replied the colonel, 'only this morning I called 'em all together and said, "The Queen's coming, boys, so you've gotta pull your socks up and be on your best behaviour. Don't swear, don't spit, and for Gawd's sake don't call me Alf."'

Busy Army doctor to recruit:
'Read the letters at the head of that chart.'
'What chart?'
'Quite right. There isn't one. You pass.'

A man, accompanied by his wife, visited a doctor's surgery and sat down, with other patients, to wait his turn. In due course he was called into the doctor's presence and his wife stayed behind in the waiting room, expecting that he would reappear in a few minutes. In fact, however, half an hour passed without his reappearance and his wife, realising that her children would soon be back from school and wanting their tea, decided to go home, after leaving a message for her husband with one of the patients. She accordingly turned to the patient (a woman) who was next in line to her, and said: 'Excuse me, do you remember what my husband looks like?'

'Good heavens!' replied the woman, 'Do you mean to say you've forgotten?'

A pushing young reporter travelling by train found himself sitting opposite an old man with rosy cheeks and luxuriant white hair; the very picture of health. Scenting a story, the reporter said: 'Pardon me, sir, I represent the *Daily Echo* and I am sure my readers would be interested to know the secret of your remarkable health.'

'Well,' said the old man in a senile treble, 'I've never had any use for doctors or social conventions. I've always eaten what I wanted to eat, drunk what I wanted to drink and done what I wanted to do.'

'And may I ask how old you are, sir?' enquired the young man eagerly.

'Certainly, certainly,' quavered the old man, 'I'm thirty-five.'

A clergyman who had just preached a sermon at Penton-ville Prison, was asked whether he found it very different from preaching in Church. 'No, he replied, 'the only real difference is that in Pentonville one preaches to convicted *criminals.'*

'What do you think of our beautiful new neighbour?'

'She is beautiful isn't she? What's more, I understand that she's a wonderful mother to her four well behaved children; a splendid cook; does all her own sewing; keeps her house like a new pin—organises marvellous parties for her husband's business friends, and is active on local committees. She makes me sick.'

A bishop about to be enthroned was standing at the entrance of his cathedral and, as is customary, knocked three times on the door with his crozier. Nothing happened immediately, but then the door opened and he was met by a procession consisting of the Dean, Sub-dean and Canons— all well stricken in years. Before they were within earshot, the bishop muttered to his chaplain, 'The See gives up its dead.'

'Is it true that you called the Seargeant-Major a —— ?'

'Yes.'

'What did he say?'

'Well, as a matter of fact, I don't think he heard me.'

A French General who had distinguished himself in the First World War was subsequently made a Marshal of France. One day, in his old age, he was distributing prizes at a French girls' school, and one of the younger pupils, on receiving her prize, curtseyed respectfully, and said:

'It is a great honour and pleasure for me to meet you again, M. le Maréchal.'

'What, my dear, said the Marshal, 'have you met me before?'

'Why yes, M. le Maréchal, in History.'

During a period of anticlericalism in France when the influence of the Church was looked upon, in certain quarters, with hostility and suspicion, the man who was later to become Marshal Petain was asked how many of his officers went to Mass. 'I can't say,' he replied, 'I always sit in the front pew.'

Before the introduction of the dinner jacket, the correct evening dress for a gentleman was tails with a white tie or, if ladies were not present, a black tie. On one occasion the compiler's father attended a dinner-party at which ladies were present, mistakenly wearing a black tie. He apologised to his hostess who immediately put him at his ease by saying, 'Never mind, Mr Edwards, you evidently don't spend much time in front of your looking glass.'

It was the junior Scripture class and the children had before them a copy of Bunyan's famous hymn from *Pilgrim's Progress*. One of the pupils read aloud the first four lines and then it was the turn of young Jane, whose practice it was, when she came across an unfamiliar word, not to spell it out, but to have a wild stab at it, hoping for the best. On this occasion she read, haltingly but correctly, the words:

> '. . . there's no discouragement
> shall make him once relent
> his first avowed intent
> to be a—'

Here she stopped short, for the word 'pilgrim' was new to her.

'Come Jane dear,' said the teacher gently, 'to be a what?'

'Please Miss,' replied Jane, adopting her usual tactics, 'a penguin.'

An old Irishman of ninety-nine was buying a new pair of shoes and insisted that, above all things, they should be durable. The shop assistant, who knew the old man's age, permitted himself a discreet smile. 'I know just what you're thinking,' said the old man. 'You're thinking I'll die before the shoes wear out. Well, let me tell you that the number of people who die over the age of ninety-nine is microscopic. You look at the statistics!'

A man and wife had gone away on holiday and had arranged for their dog to be cared for in a dog's home. When they returned from their holiday the husband collected the dog and drove home with it.

'I don't know what's the matter with him,' he said to his wife, 'he's been barking all the way home. Do you think he's homesick for the kennels?'

'No,' said his wife, 'what he's been trying to tell you is that he's the wrong dog.'

There are few European countries in whose politics women have played a more important part than France, and few French public men in France who knew this better than Napoleon. When, therefore, he was as yet only General Bonaparte, and a lady asked him what weapons he feared most, he replied, 'Fans, madam.'

Lord Melbourne, who was Prime Minister when Queen Victoria came to the throne in 1837, was asked what he thought of Thomas Macauley, the historian. He replied that he wished he could be as certain of anything as Macauley was of everything.

A little girl was asked how she had liked her first day at school.

'Not much,' she replied, 'but then I'm not very fond of children.'

From a sports report:

'When the teams turned out, there were about 12,000 spectators and large numbers were still rolling on the ground.'

Extract from speech by the headmaster of Eton, as reported in morning paper:

'They did not want to make their games a professional kind of trial, merely for the amusement of those who hardly knew one end of a football from the other.'

Extract from New Zealand paper:

'Mr P. J. Wedderspoon issued a policy statement yesterday in which he said he believed in home rule for the South Island. He said his favourite pastime was standing on a haystack abusing sheep.'

Extract from provincial paper:
'A well attended baboon dance was held in the —— Tea Rooms.'

Extract from church paper:
'The third setting to hymn 468 is most crude and I notice that the composer is still alive. Why?'

An old Irish woman, to her profound relief, had been found not guilty of keeping a dog without a licence and the magistrate told her that she was free to leave the court.
'Thank you sir,' she exclaimed, 'and God bless your Honour, and her Ladyship too, if so be there's any lady lucky enough to be married to your Majesty.'

'Do you like oysters?'
'I don't know. I've never tasted one.'
'Well taste one now.'
'No thanks, I've already got enough tastes that I can't afford to satisfy, and I don't want to acquire any more.'

' 'Tis a strange thing,' said an Irishman. 'I've never seen a man with one short leg but the other was longer.'

75

During the First World War an Irishman was asked what he thought would happen if conscription was introduced in Ireland, the whole of which was then part of the United Kingdom.

'Well,' said the man, 'speaking for myself, I'd go to war willingly if I was compelled to.'

Extract from the Essex County Standard:
'*Mrs Harrison is friendly, likeable and easy to talk to. . . . She has a fine, fair skin which, she admits ruefully, comes out in a mass of freckles at the first hint of sin.*'

From the *Birkenhead News*:
'The launching ceremony was carried out by Mrs Lill Bull, wife of Mr Christian R. Bull, and despite her giant size, she moved smoothly into the waiting waters of the Mersey.'

Seen in the Gainsborough News:
'*Hundreds of satisfied women can't be wrong: take a trip down to Fred's, 85 Trinity Street, Gainsborough.*'

A man who had spent a long time cast away on a desert island was overjoyed when he woke up one morning to see a large ship at anchor nearby. He waved frantically to attract attention and in due course a rowing boat, manned by two seamen and containing a bundle of newspapers, landed on the island.

'The Captain's compliments,' said one of them as he brought ashore the bundle of newspapers. 'We shall be staying here another two days and he thinks you might care to cast your eye over these before deciding whether or not you want to be rescued.'

A drunken Irish sailor was asked why he was walking with one foot on the pavement and the other in the gutter.

'Is that what I'm doing?' he replied. 'Thank heaven. I thought I was a cripple.'

Hostess: 'Do you really have to go?'

Guest: 'Oh no, there's no compulsion. It's purely a matter of choice.'

Meet disaster like a man and success like a gentleman.
(Anon.)

Host, having trodden on departing lady's long skirt:

'I'm terribly sorry. It must have been my subconscious mind trying to detain you.'

Advertisement in Spanish paper:

'English Spanish Shorthand Typist. Efficien. Useless. Apply Otherwise.'